BRITAIN IN OLD PHO

Sedgley, Coseley & the Gornals

TREVOR GENGE

SUTTON PUBLISHING

Sutton Publishing Limited
Phoenix Mill · Thrupp · Stroud
Gloucestershire · GL5 2BU

First published 2001

Title page: All Saints', Sedgley, seen here from the north-west through its terraced shrubbery gardens. Nineteenth-century maps show the garden site, in Gospel End Street, occupied by cottages.

British Library Cataloguing in Publication Data
A catalogue record for this book is available from the British Library.

ISBN 0-7509-2673-2

Typeset in 10.5/13.5 Photina.
Typesetting and origination by
Sutton Publishing Limited.
Printed and bound in England by
J.H. Haynes & Co. Ltd, Sparkford.

THE BLACK COUNTRY SOCIETY

This voluntary society, affiliated to the Civic Trust, was founded in 1967 as a reaction to the trend of the late 1950s and early 1960s to amalgamate everything into large units and in the Midlands to sweep away the area's industrial heritage in the process.

The general aim of the Society is to create interest in the past, present and future of the Black Country, and early on it campaigned for the establishment of an industrial museum. In 1975 the Black Country Living Museum was started by Dudley Borough Council on 26 acres of totally derelict land adjoining the grounds of Dudley Castle. This has developed into an award-winning museum which attracts over 250,000 visitors annually.

It was announced in August 1998 that having secured a lottery grant of nearly £3 million, the Museum Board will be able to authorize the start of work on a £4.5 million state-of-the-art interpretation centre. This will be known as the 'Rolfe Street Project', named after the street which once housed the Smethwick Baths. The façade of this Victorian building is to be incorporated into the new interpretation centre.

At the Black Country Living Museum there is a boat dock fully equipped to restore narrowboats of wood and iron and different vessels can be seen on the dock throughout the year. From behind the Bottle and Glass Inn visitors can travel on a canal boat into Dudley Canal Tunnel, a memorable journey to see spectacular limestone caverns and the fascinating Castle Mill Basin.

There are 2,500 members of the Black Country Society and all receive the quarterly magazine *The Blackcountryman*, of which 124 issues have been published since its founding in 1967. In the whole collection there are some 1,800 authoritative articles on all aspects of the Black Country by historians, teachers, researchers, students, subject experts and ordinary folk with an extraordinary story to tell. The whole constitutes a unique resource about the area and is a mine of information for students and researchers who frequently refer to it. Many schools and libraries are subscribers. Three thousand copies of the magazine are printed each quarter. It is non-commercial, and contributors do not receive payment for their articles.

PO Box 71 · Kingswinford · West Midlands DY6 9YN

CONTENTS

The Sedgley Parish clerk's record of the 1851 Census details showing the varied populations of the nine villages and the total population of the parish.

Mrs Golding standing outside the mill at West Coseley, 1940s. Taken before the cement rendering has been added, the picture reveals that the mill is brick-built and has received the traditional Black Country damp-proofing of gas tar. The strange upturned boat-shaped housing for the sails shafting which was shown in *Sedgley & District: A Second Selection*, p. 55, has been replaced now with a conventional hipped roof.

INTRODUCTION

This book is the fourth in a series. The first three were entitled simply *Sedgley and District* and set out to describe the once considerable extent and unique character of the area. It has been my intention throughout to create a permanent, comprehensive archive of this once great manor and parish for the benefit of modern readers; particularly, those who may live here without ever knowing anything of its history, and those who have made their homes in other places or even other countries, but for whom Sedgley remains their emotional home. I have also attempted to preserve in one collection, the evidence of the nine separate villages which formerly made up the district, and which are well represented in many of our ancient documents. I might add that the books have also allowed many people to share their personal photographic and narrative recollections to a greater or lesser extent; while others may gain a glimpse of the rich seam of historical information which lies within our local authority archives and may hopefully find encouragement to make use of these vital services for themselves.

Within this brief I have also taken the opportunity to illustrate the varied characteristics present within Sedgley: its land use and buildings; its industry, communications, people and events; its churches, shops, schools and pubs, that have often been influential centres of community life. All of these have contributed in their own way to the story. As research remains incomplete, there is still room for debate even as to whether Sedgley was first a manor or a parish. Many of the English parishes are over ten centuries old; the Domesday Book gives us the first recorded reference to a 'priest' at Sedgley in 1086. Who knows if there was one before? It is sufficient then, for the present, to regard the land areas of both the ancient manor and parish as having been the same, sharing the same boundaries, throughout the greater number of years of its undivided existence. I have also taken the opportunity to show, photographically, evidence that Sedgley was inhabited even before it got its name.

This new title, then, seeks to include, within Sedgley as a whole, the three principal named areas, two of which were reintroduced to prominence only during the recent, brief period of our history when they became urban districts. Although these may be the names people best remember, because current in their lifetime, we must note that, though important, Sedgley and Coseley Urban Districts existed as such for only seventy years out of a history that reaches back more than a thousand; and that it is now more than thirty-five years since their official demise – another very good reason for recording them here.

In each of the books I have tried to create a nostalgic, yet realistic impression of the area, recognising that not all of those times gone by were necessarily the 'good old days'. They have provided many happy experiences nonetheless, and by all accounts reliving them has encouraged some lively discussions and the sharing of memories, to many people's mutual benefit and enjoyment.

The scope of each book, and the desirability of supplementing official archive information with the many 'gems' that reside in people's family collections, has inevitably led to some variation in the amount of coverage each village has received within any one book. My aim has been to correct any such imbalance across the series, though it should be borne in mind that some villages are more populous than others, and therefore have generated more material. In some cases, too, I have had to rely entirely on the memory of the lender for the explanation that finds its way into the picture caption. The inevitable debates that follow publication may sometimes lead to alterations being made in subsequent editions, but just as often lead to the vindication of statements given in good faith. That the books provide an opportunity for scrutinizing the evidence, and sometimes for amending our conclusions, is an additional benefit for those engaged in serious research into this area. Where possible, I have given cross-references to other books in the series to provide continuity and access to additional information.

None of the books is the result of one author's efforts alone and, as always, I am grateful to those who have volunteered material, whether written or photographic. Throughout the two years I have been collecting for this book, many people have contributed either information or advice, and I have tried to acknowledge all your helpful inputs at the back of the book. Once more, I am particularly indebted to the good offices of Ron Baker and to the enthusiastic research undertaken by Margaret Roper. This time, too, I must especially mention the National Science Museum in London for permission to use their photograph of a steam tram at Fighting Cocks, which is of such excellent quality.

As always, difficult decisions have had to be made to leave perfectly good illustrations aside, perhaps until another time. That the history of Sedgley still continues to provide so much new material always comes as a welcome surprise. I am privileged indeed to be able to make so much of it available for the further interest and pleasure of the reader.

1

Streets, Roads, Lanes & Paths

A quiet scene in Catholic Lane showing one of its last surviving elms before the attack of Dutch elm disease in 1975.

The Lower Path, now almost obliterated, was an ancient footpath to the Parish Church. The remnant seen above shows it as it reaches Cinderhill, on the south side of Beacon Hill Cemetery.

The Lower Path on the south side of Lanesfield Primary School. Its name comes from the description of the two halves of the parish known for administrative convenience, as the population grew, as Upper and Lower Sedgley.

Looking north-east in 1984, Cotwall End Road looks like a rural lane. This scene must have changed little over the centuries.

Similarly, where Cotwall End Road passes through dense summer hedges, it bends and narrows near the field named Ezekiel's Piece, seen here in the 1980s. It is more suitable to slow cart traffic than the motor car.

Beacon Lane is seen here as it approaches the summit of Beacon Hill. The old hilltop cottage is to the left, and the modern telecommunications mast is on the right. The lane features in the book *Dr Bradley Remembers* by the author Frances Brett Young.

Catholic Lane with a view of the hay harvest in Cotwall End fields in the summer of 1984.

Bank Street, Coseley, 1967. On the right is the wooden hut of the British Legion, a popular venue for a variety of community uses. It was not called Bank Street because of the bank that stood off the service road for the shops of the Birmingham New Road, but because it led to Mason's Bank, the oldest hamlet of the area.

At this time Bank Street was a busy Coseley street. The public toilets stood on South Street, before the hut, while further down on this side was the private house (right) that became the Food Office during the Second World War, although the first ration books were given out from Ebenezer Sunday School, west of the Birmingham New Road. The house reverted to private use after the war, becoming the home of Pam Pit Keathly.

Looking north up Vale Street, Ruiton. Formerly known as Botany Street, as it led to a group of nine houses on the west side known as Botany Bay, and later as Vale Crest. At the time of the 1881 Census three of the houses showed the wives as nailors. We can imagine that earlier name arising from bleak conditions and the inhabitants appearing as prisoners of their circumstances.

Ruiton Street, Lower Gornal, leading from The Five Ways, the heart of Lower Gornal, to The Holloway, and from there to Vale Street, 1972.

Sandyfields Road heading towards Sedgley. It winds at this point to pass through the ancient village centre of Cotwall End, now often known as St George's after the Roman Catholic Chapel built there after the Reformation. The first mass was celebrated on St George's Day 1789. (See *Sedgley & District*, pp. 64 & 65)

Gospel End Street is often known as 'Bush Bank', a name usually attributed to The Bush Inn that once stood at the top, at the divide between Gospel End Street and Vicar Street. Where Gospel End Street commences at the point of its junction with Gospel End Road and Cotwall End Road is a village boundary, and another is reached just along Cotwall End Road. The names 'Bush Bank' and 'Bush Inn' may refer to an even earlier landmark as thorn bushes and notable trees often provided good boundary markers.

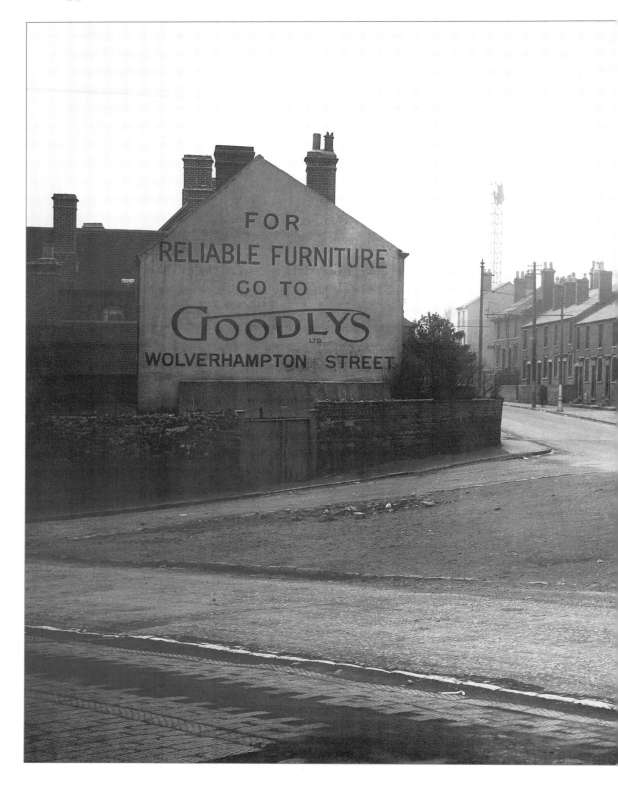

The southern boundary of the manor is here at the junction of Dibdale Road, left, with the Wolverhampton Streetways Turnpike, now Highland Road. Salop Street marks the entrance to Dudley. A filling station today occupies the site of the house advertising a Dudley furniture shop and its neighbour. The cross on the wall, centre, probably indicates that some of these houses and shops are actually on a narrow tongue of land belonging to Dudley. Everything to the left of the cross is in Sedgley, though it is not so on the other side of the road which from Dibdale Road is all in Upper Gornal.

In the late 1920s Coseley began building a housing scheme at Lanesfield. The Birmingham New Road had been opened in November 1927 and Ward Grove became one of the roads running off at right angles. The abrupt end at a hedge and the fields rolling downwards from Sedgley Beacon shows the first extent of this estate, or 'scheme', as it was known.

Bank Street, Coseley, seen nearing Castle Street and the Square, 1967. On the north-east side was the office of R. Jackson, builder, The chainyard and the rear of George Mason's can also be seen.

A scene of Gospel End, early in the twentieth century. The old post office on the left presents a picture of rural charm. The same view photographed eighty years later (below) shows a well-lit main road from Wombourne and the Stourbridge Road to Sedgley. The post office and its cottages, together with many other older dwellings, have gone.

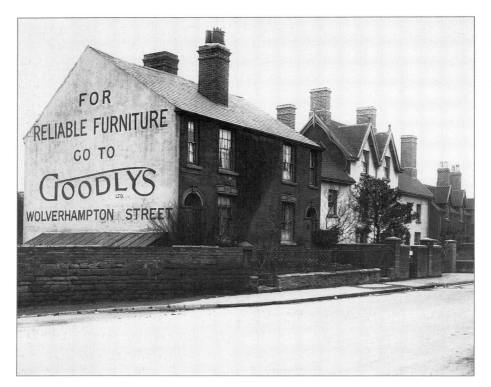

This 1920s picture shows the front of the houses on page 14 that were demolished for the filling station.

The eastern side of Highland Road shows the varied nature of dwellings that sprang up along the old turnpike road.

A 1960s picture of Vale Street, Upper Gornal, as it reaches the Ridgeway at the Moden Hill crossing. The name Ridgeway is appropriate because of its consistency to the line of an old footpath or bier way to All Saints' Church, from Lower Gornal.

Clarence Street, Upper Gornal, in the 1960s when change had begun. Again part of the old turnpike route, there are modern houses now on the left while older houses still stand, right. The large distant building on the left is Mount Zion Methodist Church before demolition.

This view shows the High Street at Sedgley, with the house of Hilton the local builder on the left, and the gardens of what was called the Manor House, but never was. To the right is the forecourt of the Red Lion Inn. The scene was probably photographed by Mr Egginton, the chemist, in 1910.

A drawing by artist and historian Andrew Barnett gives a valuable view of 1948 showing the top of the Lower Path (see page 8) at Cinderhill as it approaches Homer's Barn opposite the Talbot Inn, and gives a glimpse of Bath Street beyond. The Beacon slopes are seen to the right.

Bilston Street, Sedgley, from the High Street, possibly 1960s. The houses and cottages on the right were demolished in the 1970s, and on the left not all of the row are retailers. This row is now safely within a conservation area. The steeple in the distance is that of Bilston Street Congregational Church, now renamed St Andrew's URC/Methodist.

Bilston Street looking towards the High Street in 1975. The terraced blocks, seen right, have all now been replaced by new housing.

Commendably, these houses in Highland Road, Upper Gornal, photographed here in the 1920s, have recently been refurbished and maintain their sturdy presence on the streetscape.

The shape of things to come! This 1960s picture shows civil work underway at the commencement of the development of The Northway estates. The wooded ridge of Kinsell, anciently King's Hill, is seen at the rear.

2

Farms & Farming

Conqueror's Farm, Lower Gornal stood on Cotwall End Road, nearing Straits Green, and backing on to the southern end of The Dingle, now part of the Cotwall End Nature Reserve.

A summer view into Cotwall End and to Wood Farm from the boundary footpath with Gospel End. The stable block in the foreground shows the modern use of fields for the grazing and sheltering of horses in private ownership, and other equestrian activities.

KNOWN AS

WOOD FARM, GOSPEL END

WITH A GOOD HOUSE AND EXCELLENT FARM BUILDINGS,

having access roads from **Gospel End Road** and **Sandyfields Road,** within a mile from the centre of Sedgley.

Area, 104a. 0r. 4p. or thereabouts

THE HOUSE, at present converted into two dwellings, is substantially built in brick with a tiled roof and is located at a convenient distance from the Buildings.   The Accommodation comprises:—

On the Ground Floor :—Two Living Rooms, Kitchen, Scullery with sink, two Pantries, Dairy and Washhouse.

On the First Floor :—Four good Bedrooms, also three Attic Bedrooms.

Main Water supply is installed.   Paved House Yard with usual outbuildings and e.c.

THE FARM BUILDINGS are well arranged around a stock yard and are most substantially built in brick with tiled roofs—they have been maintained to a high standard and include:—Two Barns, 21-tie Cowhouse, two four-stall Stables, three Loose Boxes, Feeding Shed, Cowhouse for 9 cows, and three-bay Feeding Shed.

Adjacent to these Buildings is the Rickyard with five-bay Dutch Barn and a three-bay steel and corrugated iron Implement Shed.

Let to Mr. H. G. Jenkins on an annual Ladyday tenancy, at an apportioned rent of **£98. 6s. 0d.** per annum.

SCHEDULE.

O.S. No.	Description.				Area. Acres.	O.S. No.	Description.				Area. Acres.
	Parish of Sedgley.						Brought forward			...	54·747
414	Pasture	...	...	...	5·094	472	Pasture	...	...	...	2·722
420	Arable	...	...	...	6·731	473	Pasture	...	...	...	1·256
425	Pasture	...	...	...	4·506	474	Pasture	...	...	...	7·428
Pt. 462	Pasture	...	...	...	·369	475	Arable	...	...	...	7·928
465	Arable	...	...	...	7·191	541	Arable	...	...	...	5·044
466	Arable	...	...	...	3·254	542	Slang and Drive		...	...	·554
467	Pasture	...	...	...	3·552	544	Arable	...	...	...	6·513
468	House, Buildings, etc.			...	2·702	547	Arable	...	...	...	12·535
469	Pasture	...	...	...	13·096	Pt. 548	Pasture	...	...	...	1·845

In 1947 many of the Earl of Dudley's holdings were made available for sale. Here is the Wood Farm catalogue entry showing the field use having a higher proportion of arable land than pasture.

A late afternoon view of some of the outbuildings and yard of Spout House Farm, Cotwall End Road, some thirty years ago. Today the buildings are derelict and awaiting either restoration, or new development of the site.

Spout House Farm, 1947. The farm probably got its name from the almost continuous supply of water arising from springs in this area. An ancient watermill, whose 'quern' or millstone probably gave Gornal its name, used the same supply many centuries before, a little way south-east of the farm.

These dairy cattle, probably an Ayrshire cross breed, were photographed on The Rough, off Cinder Road, Lower Gornal, in the 1950s. The railway that ran through Gornal Halt station is seen in the background.

Here, by contrast, at Red Lane Farm in the year 2000 are a Belgian Blue and a Charollais.

A young Roger Wooldridge gets a feel for the tractor at the family farm at Sandyfields, Lower Gornal, in the 1960s. This practice may soon be banned under European legislation.

A barn with dovecote, and the distant farmhouse at Sandyfields, Cotwall End. The farm once stood on Sandyfields Road until a sharp bend was straightened and the old road was left as a service road to the farm.

Arable crops, like this field of barley growing in Calves Croft, Cotwall End, in 1972, were evident in the parish well beyond the Second World War. In 1843 Stephen Law, a descendant of a notable Sedgley recusant family, was farming this field.

Crossing to the east of the ridge to Turls Hill, actually in the old village of Ettingshall, we find another typical agricultural scene, and beyond are the white scars of the Wrens Nest limestone, in Woodsetton.

A sad picture of Gospel End farmhouse, demolished in error in 1966. It can be seen as the distinguished building it was in *Sedgley & District*, p. 42.

Alongside the stone barn of the farm this old hay tedder stood idle for many months, photographed here in the 1960s. Pulled by horses its tines turned and spread the hay. It was hard work for the horses in hot summer weather.

Sedgley has always benefited from numerous springs, brooks, and many dewponds. This one was once part of Gospel End Farm lands and its water level still fluctuates dramatically in summer.

Two enormous stone barns once served Cotwall End House. The dovecote apertures also indicate the age of the barns, and their doors are capable of admitting tall loaded haywains. A surviving barn still stands.

Local pastures still yield prolifically, as shown by this field in Gospel End, seen during a recent summer. Today only horses graze it, though in 1843 it was part of the landholdings of the Wilkes family. Stephen Wilkes, the Nail Master, was using it, though Martin Wilkes owned it.

Artist and historian Andrew Barnett has captured the 'Spirit of Haymaking' in this impression of the Whitwell field, Cotwall End.

A survivor of different times, this house in Gorge Road was Hurst Hill Farm, and would have used the land now occupied by the Gorge Estate. See also page 125.

This house began life as stone built, but its walls have been extended upwards in brick. Photographed here in the 1990s it was present on the Tithe Map of 1843 and still remains today. Was it once the home for several farm workers that became one house? The house visible at the rear right is The Laurels.

3

Houses Great & Small

A drawing of the Post Office cottages in Gospel End by Ron Davies. It may be compared with the photograph on page 65.

This brick cottage in Straits Green, Gornal Wood, seems to face west, as did many more in The Straits. Like this one, their windows were all on the 'front' of the house, even though in some cases that would present a blank wall to the road. It seemed to be a local practice to build houses in this manner, facing the afternoon and evening sun.

Straits Green Road, Lower Gornal, 1930s. This stone cottage was the home of Anne Marie Southall (seated left) with two of her children, Alice May Fellows (standing) and Doris Parkes (seated). The cottage was later renumbered 77 Cotwall End Road.

Ron Baker provides an interesting drawing to show this house and its neighbour in Gospel End Street. They would eventually become the pet shop, featured on pages 60 and 61, but by this time the two were linked.

This photograph, taken from the back garden of the cottage above, shows both the link building, and the outhouses.

The Straits House, Lower Gornal, is now an inn of the same name, but in this 1947 photograph the premises were still in private hands.

The Firs, Wodehouse Road, Gospel End, now a nursing home, but seen here in 1947 still privately owned.

Bunkers Hill House, was the home of Joseph Smith, first clerk of Coseley Urban District Council. Some idea of the status of the occupant can be seen from this view in Tipton Street, showing the stables and carriage house, the mark of a gentleman. Notice also the typical pitching ring for hay to be thrown through into the loft.

Cartwright's Newsagents, Dudley Street, Sedgley, seen from Egginton's. It is believed that Cartwright had a house in Dean Street (formerly Church Street) with a long garden reaching to the turnpike road at Dudley Street. He simply built his shop in the garden to accept the new opportunities that a busier Dudley Street provided.

A fine pair of 'status' houses in the Georgian style in Dudley Road, Sedgley, 1970.

Another Georgian house in Gospel End showing blind windows to avoid Window Tax, which was not abolished until 1851. This photograph shows the building converted to semi-detached. It was demolished for the rebuilding of most of Gospel End Village in about 1976.

Ebenezer Street, Coseley. A mixture of housing styles showing individual developments during the nineteenth century, probably replacing even older properties. The street takes its name from the Ebenezer Baptist Church, to which it leads. Though cut now by the Birmingham New Road, a fragment remains by the church.

This block of artisan dwellings in High Holborn, Sedgley, appears here to be in a state of dereliction. Fortunately it was restored, and still survives as a typical early Victorian terrace block with no front gardens.

An interesting illustration of the effect of demolition on the streetscape is provided by these two photographs. The houses next to the Sedgley Council House drive were demolished in the late 1960s to make way for the access and car park for the supermarket. Only the tree remains to provide an impression of height.

These houses along Sandyfields Road, Cotwall End, help to make up the pretty hamlet of St George's, which was probably the centre of old Cotwall End Village. The name St George's comes from the small Roman Catholic chapel, built here in 1782 and dedicated to St George. It was consecrated on St George's Day with a mass that included prayers for the ailing King George. The houses, though constantly refurbished over the years, could date from the seventeenth century, or possibly even earlier.

This house went by the name of Wilson's Hill Farm. It stood off High Park Crescent, Sedgley, enjoying the panoramic views towards Shropshire and beyond. It was demolished in 2001. Its last occupant was Joan Simner.

A picture postcard of Sedgley Hall in snow. The Hall was featured in *Sedgley & District* on page 15. It had its origins in the sixteenth century and was demolished in 1966, in preparation for Sedgley Hall Estate.

St Peter's Church House. This attractive house with its mullioned windows stood in Kent Street, Upper Gornal, next to St Peter's church until the 1960s. At one time it was the home of the Raybould family, who were closely attached to the church and its life. Another family were the Wall family with their four daughters. The photograph was taken in the 1930s.

This tiny cottage in Bank Road, Lower Gornal, photographed in 1967 makes a striking contrast to the dwellings on the following page!

Even in its ruined state there is no disguising the splendour of the castle at Dudley photographed here in about 1900. The whole scene was contained within the southern extremity of the village of Woodsetton, until the late 1920s.

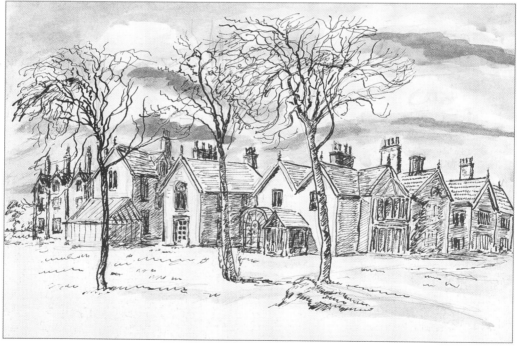

There is little trace of Turls Hill house today, lying along White's Drive. It is shown here in a sketch by Andrew Barnett, who probably used the opportunity of the snow glow to create this bright scene of buildings that were most often shadowed by trees. Its most prolific builder seems to have been Ben Whitehouse, of the famous family of ironmasters, whose work is shown on page 75.

No. 8 High Holborn. This gracious Georgian house must have been home to several families throughout its life. Again, the coach entrance gives an indication of wealth. Its last occupant was Mrs B. Watkins. The photograph dates from the late 1960s.

The scene today shows the Holborn Centre that now occupies the site. The tree reminds us of its relationship to the old house.

This is the rear elevation of 8 High Holborn, the house shown on page 45.

Cottages next to the Woodman Inn, Wakelem's Fold, Lower Gornal, 1967. The nailshop on the right was shown in *Sedgley & District* on page 33.

This house stands at the end of Beacon Street, Cinderhill, where it joins Woodcross Lane. Dovedale Road, seen left, was just a farm lane leading to Ettingshall Park Farmhouse. The house was once the home of Coseley Councillor Joseph Pugh (seen amid the group in *Sedgley & District* on page 118.) Pugh Road in Woodcross took its name from him. Later years saw a period when more than one family occupied the house. Now the house is restored and stands as the only survivor of its once many neighbours.

Many Sedgley folk took recreation from walking the field paths of the parish where it was not unusual to find the occasional house built in a quite isolated situation. Many older walkers around Baggeridge will remember the White Houses, seen here in a state of dereliction, on their walk towards Wombourne.

More dereliction is seen here in the heart of Sedgley, early 1970s, when Dean Street was demolished. Old Dean Street (formerly Church Street) was a mixture of two-storey, both brick and stone cottages, together with a three-storey Georgian brick built house (seen in *Sedgley & District*) while at the junction with Vicar Street stood the parish vestry room. (*Sedgley & District: A Second Selection*)

4

Churches
& Chapels

Tipton Street Primitive Methodist Chapel is seen here in this early twentieth-century postcard. It has a pleasing front elevation set off by its young trees and ornamental railings and gates. As a Grade II listed building its value to the local streetscape is obvious.

An interior view of the Roman Catholic Church of St Chad and All Saints, Sedgley. It dates from before the photograph shown in *Sedgley & District*, as the lancet windows in the chancel were not completed until 1914. The wall decoration shows that the window apertures were originally left blind.

All Saints Parish Church, clergy and choir, 1939.

Kent Street Wesley, Upper Gornal, often held their Sunday School 'treat' day at the home of Mr Howl, at The Quarries. Here a group of the menfolk, soon to engage in bowls on the lawn, sit with the host. Standing, left to right: W.H. Potts, E. Caddick, J. Harris, H. Baker, A. Bennett, L. Hyde (Sen.) F. Porter. Seated: B. Price, Mr R. Howl, H. Bennett and L. Hyde (Jnr) in front.

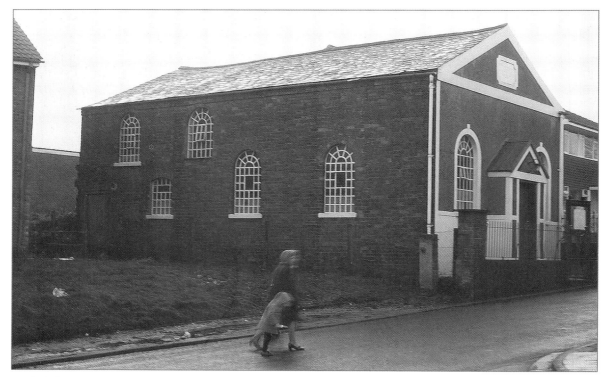

Cinderhill Methodist Church closed its doors for the last time after the Harvest Festival of the year 2000, bringing to an end 150 years of service to the hamlet.

Gornal Wood, seen from the playing fields in the 1960s, has the steeple of Zoar Methodist Church topping the scene like a parish church.

Upper Ettingshall Methodist Youth Club perform *The Shining Way* in 1944. The cast are back row, left to right, Kenneth Raybould, William Davies, Austin Jarrott, Stanley Atwell. Third row: Doreen Astley, Kathleen Jarrott (leader), Ethel Jarrott, Nellie Jones, Eileen Shelley, Thelma Griffiths, Sheila Fellows, Jean Cox, Eileen Simner. Second row: Iris Webb, Sheila Irving, Beryl Hickman, Greta Cox, Rita Harper, Thelma Holcroft, Maureen Jones, Sylvia Powell. Front row: -?-, -?-, ? Hickman, Alan Fellows and Arnold Powell.

A ceramic mural celebrating the union of the Bilston Street Congregational Church and the High Street Methodist Church in 1970. It is situated in the new vestibule of the succeeding St Andrew's URC/Methodist Church in Bilston Street. The mural by William H. Burgess depicts both churches and their settings in the community of Sedgley, together with glimpses of local industries and the fossils and flora of Sedgley Beacon.

Lanesfield Methodist Youth Club in 1950s. Back row, left to right: Elsie Clarke, Eileen Bull, Vida Walford, Rita Burton, Sylvia Fellows, Sheila Burton, Joan Bradford, Beryl Amos, Barbara Charlesworth, Marjorie Littlewood, Sheila Flavell, Pauline Caine, Beryl Griffiths, Vilma Whitehouse, Iris Saunders, Wendy Turner. Third row: Pat Cornfield, -?- , Kathleen Braden, Barbara Bate, -?-, George Bunce, Ken Smith, Bert Ferrier, Jack Bennett, Derek Boulton, Terry Duncombe, John Bunce, Terry Hampton, Ken Tucker, -?-. Second row: Iris Astley, Mary Griffiths, Alma Thomas, Nora Darlington, -?-, Christine Deakin, Linda Whitehouse, Olive Lee, Nora Vaughan, Mary Briscoe, Howard Briscoe, Norman Smith, Clarice Smith, Doris Whitehouse, Alma Price, Rita Clarke, Margaret Meredith. Front row: Maurice Hill, Bob Dudley, -?-, Jimmy Turner, Gordon Fellows, Alan Edwards, Ernie Noakes, Trevor Genge, Derek Noakes, Billy Griffiths, Roy Purnell.

Kent Street Wesleyan Sunday School 'treat' day at The Quarries, Upper Gornal. Pictured here is the children's tea in 1935.

The bowls match at The Quarries in full flow. Seen are W.H. Potts, H. Baker and the onlooker (right) is H. Bennett. This is from the same 1935 event. See also page 51.

5

Shops & Services

Sedgley Pets, later Precisely Pets, in Gospel End Street (see drawing on page 35). In 2001 the shop began retailing again, though the new owners now offer homeopathic medicines.

This butcher's shop was at Five Ways, Lower Gornal, next to the Five Ways Inn. The staff seen are of the Cornmell family. On the left is an interesting playbill for Dudley Opera House. No date is given, but it would appear to date from the early 1900s. It advertises a varied programme, twice nightly at 7 p.m. and 9 p.m. Appearing were: Battling Bantam, The Great Little Hackenshmidt, 'CHYTO', Anderson, Jackson & Law, Olive Marshall, Ernie Bewsey, Leon Florence Cody, and all for 1s 9d, 6d and 4d.

Marsh's first butcher's shop at the Grand Junction Inn. This first shop was replaced by a self-contained house and shop on the opposite side of High Holborn in 1872. Many butchers shops were built next to local inns, and when they are a part of the same building one wonders about some previous influence from the 'Truck System', where workers in the nail industry were often paid in goods from 'The Master's' shops! This first shop must date from before 1879.

Sedgley post office, on its second site in the village, quite early in the twentieth century. Its staff were featured in *Sedgley & District*. This view shows it set between private residences in the High Street. Bourne House, to the left, seems to have taken its name from the sub-postmaster.

This photograph taken in 2001 shows the entire row still intact, though slightly modified, and serving different purposes. Protected by conservation area status, it should remain.

Sedgley Pets and Aquatics in 1980 when in the hands of D. Thomas. Its construction from two cottages has been shown on page 57. The address is 79 and 80 Gospel End Street.

The inside of the pet shop reveals how the proprietor catered for the widest possible variety of pets in the area, including horses. The shop provided a sight for potential customers not to be forgotten, and rather fondly remembered. It closed as a pet shop in the year 2000.

Another view of the interior of the pet shop. Almost every pet imaginable must be catered for in this Aladdin's Cave!

This photograph, taken in the early 1920s, shows Miss Lavinia Worton in front of her parents' shop (Mr and Mrs T. Worton) in Hill Street, Ruiton, Upper Gornal. The shop provided almost everything the people of Ruiton needed from the cradle to the grave. This even included corn, oats and bran for the horses of the local travelling rock salt sellers. Behind the shop was a workshop where Mr Worton made coffins for his undertaking business. It is said that, as a young man living in Ruiton Street, Lower Gornal, he began making small wooden coffins as he was so much saddened by the varied containers used for the burial of children at the time.

In late Georgian times this row in Sedgley Bullring would have been quite elegant private residences. This fine photograph shows them already in the process of changing to shops, which they now all are. While the houses thankfully survive, it is a shame that the window panes in the upper floors were changed at a time when uniformity was not insisted upon.

Kent Street, near St Peter's Church, Upper Gornal, before redevelopment. The photograph, probably taken in 1961, shows the drapery shop left and the baby linen shop two doors down. At the drapery shop door are Mrs Lucy Fithern, Mrs Wheeler, and Miss Sally Marsh.

Sedgley Bullring has long been the centre of local trade and this photograph from the 1970s shows the length of Dudley Street, from the Bullring to the Grand Junction, as a thriving hub of the community. Egginton's chemist shop lies beyond the roundabout.

An older photograph of the Bullring, looking north and showing the Red Lion. The two shops on the right are part of the block shown on page 63. Making the photograph even more interesting is the fact that it was almost certainly taken by Mr J.T. Egginton, the chemist, probably early in the twentieth century. Egginton's shop is shown in the previous picture.

Gospel End had its own sub-post office for many years. It was lost during the demolition and rebuilding of the old village. The first photograph (right) shows the Stainton family gathered outside and the second (below) the post office alongside the cottages sketched by Ron Davies and shown on page 33. The cottages are recalled particularly for a splendid display of roses each year.

Fred Williams Cycles is well known for its shops in Wolverhampton and Dudley. It all began in an old weighbridge in Dock Meadow Drive, Lanesfield, where Fred, seen standing in the doorway, carried out repairs. Fred proved particularly useful to the many workmen cycling along Spring Road in those years, often mending their punctures during the dinner hour.

One of the few corner shops surviving at the corner of Turl Street and Tipton Street, Sedgley, in the year 2000. Several attempts have been made to keep it open though most recent attempts seem short lived.

6

Public Houses

The Old Mill, in Windmill Street, Ruiton, Upper Gornal.
Peter Oliver and friend stand outside the building that
preserves in name the presence of Ruiton's first
windmill nearby.

"THE LIMERICK" INN,

UPPER GORNAL,

By order of the Trustees of the late Mr. ROWLAND HUGHES to close the Estate.

Lot 2.—The

VALUABLE FREEHOLD FULL-LICENSED HOUSE,

Known as "THE LIMERICK" INN,

Situate at Upper Gornal, on the main Wolverhampton and Dudley Road, with the Brewhouse, Stabling, and other Outbuildings, Yard, Garden, &c. ; the whole occupying an area of 812 square yards or thereabouts.

The House has excellent accommodation for a large trade, comprising :—on the **ground floor,** Passage with side entrance. large Taproom, Parlour, Bar, Pantry, Club Room. and Kitchen. with Oven and Boiler ; on the first floor, a large Club Room, Four Bedrooms, and a Spirit Room; and there are extensive Cellars in the basement.

There is a large Brewhouse with Malt Room over, and the Outbuildings comprise **Piggeries** and Boiler, Stable and Cow-house, with Loft over, &c.

The Water supply is ample, there being a capital Well, and a large Soft-water Cistern.

For many years there has been carried on a large and profitable Home-brewing business, the house being in a thickly populated district.

A purchaser will be required to take to at a valuation, in the usual way, the Brewing Plant, and Public-House Fixtures, Fittings, &c.

Solicitor :—Mr. W. A. FOSTER, Queen Street, Wolverhampton.

For further Particulars, apply to the respective SOLICITORS, or to the AUCTIONEERS,

25, Darlington Street, Wolverhampton (Telephone 7,096).

The Limerick Inn, Kent Street, Upper Gornal, came up for sale on Wednesday 19 May 1897. The sale notice makes interesting reading, particularly the bid noted in the top corner by a Mr Hanson. The Limerick was demolished with many other buildings during the rebuilding of Kent Street.

Many local inns took the name of the tradespeople who provided most of their custom. This is another Kent Street pub, the Bricklayers Arms, early in 1903, when Harry Hammond was the licensee. Now, like its neighbour, The Limerick, it has been demolished. Along the road in Sedgley was the Shinglers Arms, now the White Horse, where presumably the roof tilers drank. A new inn in Roseville carries the old name of the Chain Yard.

The Jolly Crispin in Clarence Street is one of Upper Gornal's surviving old beer houses, and is seen here in 1970.

Not to be outdone by the churches many local pubs held their own harvest festivals, and sometimes invited local clergy to perform a short thanksgiving service. Here is the array of harvest gifts, and below, the host auctions off produce for charity.

Another lost inn. This Great Western was in Bradley's Lane, Coseley, until around 1995. It certainly outlived the railway it was named after. That had ceased to pass under the road nearby since Dr Beeching's reform. The Great Western Inn was destroyed by fire after lying empty for some time.

The Yew Tree in New Street, Lower Gornal, 1960s.

A fascinating view of the Red Lion in its setting within the Bull Ring, Sedgley. This between the wars scene shows the inn yard from coaching days and two single deck buses of the old Midland Red.

The Grand Junction, High Holborn, Sedgley, retains its interesting yard with stables, pitching ring and coach house. Behind the gate on the left we can see the wall and roof of the butcher's shop featured on page 58.

7

The Industrial Past

An old nail workshop still standing between Dudley Street and Dean
Street, Sedgley, *c.* 1970.

A row of nailshops in Brick Street, Sedgley, being demolished.

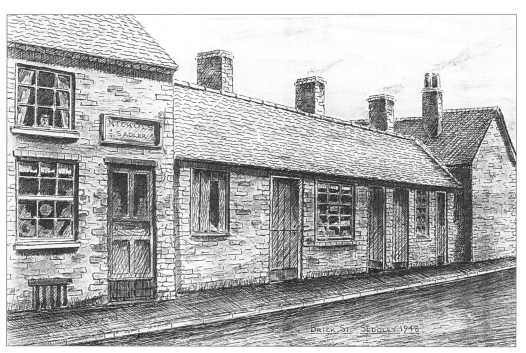

Ron Baker's drawing of the same buildings in the 1950s shows that they had been converted to other uses after the forges were closed.

Henry Bickerton Whitehouse's ironworks at Deepfields, Coseley. The Whitehouse family, originally of Brierley Hill, settled in Sedgley and for a number of years held interests in coal, ironstone, ironworking, and a little farming: they must have lived in some style. The ironworks went out of blast before the First World War. The chimney bricks and others from the site went into the building of houses on either side of Bowen Avenue, Lanesfield, reaching almost to Bate Street on the left and to Rookery Drive on the right.

In their heyday Whitehouse's provided the cannon foundry with its iron. The two works were close together. Here the old cannon warehouse, Havacre Lane, Coseley, seen in *Sedgley & District* on page 38, now lies devastated in 1981 after its clearance following a fire.

A cleared area around King Street, Coppice, shows the old screw factory of Messrs Rose, which later became Coppice Bakery. The Roses had the distinction of one member of the family being the music hall artist Clarkson Rose.

An old weighbridge that stood by James Bates' brickworks and John Norton's foundry, Spring Road/Manor Road, Lanesfield, Ettingshall, in the late 1950s. The presence of so many weighbridges, including public ones, is often forgotten today, but they were an important feature.

Harper's quarry in Ruiton developed sandstone
extraction to the point of providing a very
effective ganister for industrial furnace linings,
while still retaining the original stone getting.
Here Mrs Lucy Harper, back to camera and
sporting a locally preferred sacking apron (or
bagapron), speaks with a neighbour.

Near to Waterfield's factory was one that
turned stone back to sand, as had previously
been done by horse mill grinding.

The grim face of dereliction as the Burton Road gin pit lies disused among its spoil, with the Union workhouse behind, 1920s. Later Burton Road hospital developed here, and now a new private housing estate covers most of the cleared site.

This combined coal and clay working site was near to Woodsetton Farm, to the east of Burton Road. The photograph is thought to have been taken in the 1920s.

This picture of Baggeridge colliery, Gospel End, is from a postcard and probably dates from around 1930. In many areas of the Black Country both beauty and prestige were often gained from industrial enterprise and the edifices it created.

A scene of industrial extraction activity in the Red Bull and graveyard areas of Lower Gornal, 1960s. The former name probably arose from the local Red Cow Inn, and 'graveyard' because of an early non-conformist cemetery said to have been in this area. Today the area is better known as Grosvenor Road.

The famous Black Country 'Ten Yard Coal Seam' runs out in the west of the parish. The fault at Turner's Hill, seen here, marks a point on the Russell's Hall fault.

Two industrial casualties of the millennium. Hopyard foundry at Siddons Road, Coseley, took its name from Hopyard colliery whose site it occupied. The foundry closed in 2000 and was cleared for housing in 2001.

The second termination came for Hermit Industries, Holloway Street, Lower Gornal, whose plant was closed in 1999 and was later demolished.

A group of John Thompson apprentices after receiving their indentures in 1952. Standing, left to right: Mr W.L. Roden (supervisor), Stan Robbins, Wilf Large, Brian Higgins, Lou Willis, Ray Longstaff, Tom Walters, ? Bowman, John Bytheway. Kneeling: Chris Everitt, ? Yates.

It is often forgotten how local factories once dominated the skyline. Here in Lanesfield in the 1980s the British Steel plant at Bilston with the tall *Elisabeth* furnace stands above all else.

In Tipton Street, very close to the centre of Sedgley, are two obvious workshops. Job Horton's builders yard and DIY centre stands next to Tipton Street Chapel, while further left is Beacon Engineering, once the maker of iron bedsteads, but still manufacturing.

This picture of Coseley canal tunnel entrance is included as a reminder of the extent of the manual work that must have been involved in making its deep cutting, of those who used it and maintained it. Originally Thomas Telford intended a cutting all of its length, which would have divided the centre of Coseley. The position of the old houses seen in Ivy House Lane in 1970, would have been precarious too.

8

School &
School Life

Red Hall Elementary School infants at play. The apparatus
provided seems surprising for so early in the twentieth century.

The Red Hall schools stand on either side of Zoar Street in Gornal Wood where they have served the children of the area for over 100 years. Seen here in the 1960s, the Infant School gets a load of bricks, perhaps for modifications. Their premises were built for the Senior School children, until the new schools like Ellowes were constructed.

The Red Hall Junior School stands just across the road making moving up an easy matter. In fact the school formerly housed both Infant and Junior children.

Red Hall Infant School staff, *c.* 1900. They would have been on the other side of the road from the Junior School. The headmistress, seated prominently, is Mrs Potts.

Tudor School. Upper Gornal, with their string orchestra in the early part of the twentieth century. Their headmaster, left, is Mr W.H. Potts and the music teacher, right, is Mrs M. Mills. Music and the playing of instruments were highly regarded in the early days of public education.

...nday
Augst 41th

I, Hannah Thompson, being appointed Mistress of the Lanesfield Board School was present when Mr Hughes Chairman opened it to-day for first time, I had a good attendance, there being 80 present. On account of the age of some of the Children the Members of the Sedgley School Board think it desirable to form a Standard I Class as there is no other school very near.

Augst 15
Friday

The number of Children has varied from 80 to 87 during the week, they have been rather unruly from running the streets but are improving.
Did not enter all names till I knew how the Board had decided about the Standard I Class.
Forgot to mention that Mr Greenway was here on the Monday morning, also Mr Lane, & in the afternoon Mr Lane came with two of the members of the Board.

Tuesday
Aug 19th

The number of attendances falling off on account of irregularity. Mr Lane came

The very first page in the school log book of Lanesfield Board School in Wood Street, makes interesting reading. The headmistress, Hannah Thompson has added some comments of her own, and above all describes the new children graphically as 'unruly from running the streets'. The date at the top of the page was Monday 11 August and the year 1877. At this time it was the only school in the Lanesfield area. The school would have been labelled Sedgley Board School, and the members of the board are her first week's visitors.

Broad Lanes Secondary School, Ladymoor, on fire in 1982. It survived, to be used by Bilston College, but has recently been put up for sale, and awaits development.

The rear of Sedgley National Schools photographed before demolition in the 1960s. The supermarket and its adjoining shops on Dudley Street now occupy the front of the school site and the small car park now reaches Dean Street. The school is featured in *Sedgley & District* on page 106.

Lanesfield Primary School staff pose outside the old Wood Street School, 1953/4. Standing: D.J. Hopkins BA, Mr Victor Morris. Seated: Mrs Phyllis Foy, Ray Wearing (headmaster), Mrs Dorothy Sloan.

Lanesfield schoolchildren perform their Christmas concert in the new school, 1980s.

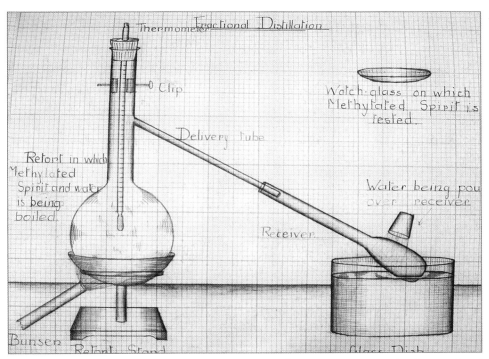

A memento of past schooldays is Harry Jevon's excellent science exercise book page dated 1924/5. Here, 'Ex.' was a most coveted assessment.

In 1965 children of Alder Coppice Primary School, Sedgley, undertake a shallow archaeological dig on the site of Sedgley Hall, with the assistance of history students and staff from Wolverhampton Day Training College for Teachers.

J.T. Homer of Dormston House inspecting one of the local Board Schools, Queen Victoria, Sedgley. He also visited the Upper Gornal schools This is obviously a playground activity staged for parents, probably on May Day. The mothers' hats suggest a date around 1928, but the event could be later.

9

Transport

A Baggeridge coal train sketched by Andrew Barnett.

A wonderful picture of a steam tram on the border of Wolverhampton and Sedgley, at the Fighting Cocks; a date between 1896 and 1901 has been suggested. This photograph, published by permission of the Science Museum, London, shows a Kitson locomotive and Starbuck trailer, both built in 1885.

In 1901 an electric service was provided, travelling through Dudley and Sedgley and turning at the Fighting Cocks for Bilston and Willenhall. Interestingly the block of property seen on the left of both pictures is still standing.

The gentleman seated in his motor car is Lieutenant Colonel Naylor of Bleak House, Upper Gornal. His chauffeur stands nearby. This must have been an early car on the Sedgley scene. In 1904 Colonel Naylor is recorded as living in Cotwall End so the photograph must date from a little later.

This scene shows admiring friends gathering around a car that probably had a connection with the Newey family, proprietors of Summit Garage, 1930s.

The quiet canal scene reveals the end of an era for the busy Black Country canals of the Industrial Revolution. This bridge was near the old Anchor Inn at Deepfields and crosses the old James Brindley line of 1777, as it turns east.

The new Anchor bridge seen crossing the Telford Canal at Coseley, as it heads south for the tunnel, also shown in *Sedgley & District: A Second Selection* on page 100. This photograph was taken in the 1980s. Telford's new line opened through the tunnel in 1837.

A modern bungalow and house with an angled rear access identify the position of an old canal arm. The scene is in Vicarage Road West, Woodsetton, Coseley.

Tom Roberts on his Ariel outside Woodbank House, Cotwall End. Tom was the last occupant of the house that was also featured in *Sedgley & District: A Second Selection*, on pages 32–33.

The GWR Kingswinford branch line lay west of the Lower Gornal border, but the pagoda-like shelters, seen either side of the track, are at Gornal Halt. The photograph dates from 1967.

On the east of the parish the Oxford, Worcester and Wolverhampton line from Dudley passed through Wallbrook and on through Brierley and Bradley. The company was later integrated into the GWR. Here, following Dr Beeching's report, the track has gone, and the bridge at Brierley Lane crosses the empty cutting.

The Stour Valley Line entered the parish at Coseley, and passed through Ettingshall on its way to Wolverhampton. It belonged to the LNWR and later the LMS railway. This is the only one of Sedgley's lines to survive, though not without alteration. In this recent scene a motor car repair workshop uses the stables and railway cart sheds of the first Coseley and Deepfields Station at the Deepfields end of Havacre Lane.

Nature reclaims the old OW&W line at Wallbrook near where the Great Western Inn (featured on page 71) stood on the road above.

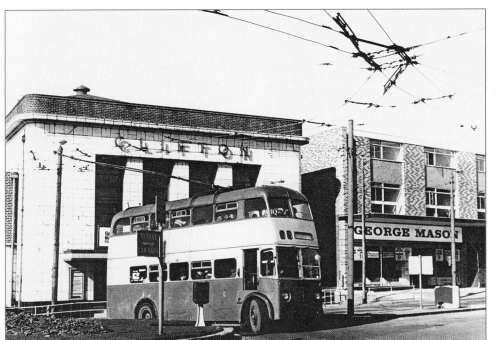

Trolley-buses can now only be seen locally at the Black Country Living Museum. Here, a Wolverhampton Corporation trolley-bus negotiates the Sedgley Bullring island, late 1960s.

The Gorge garage and filling station awaits clearance for modern houses. Roadside filling stations are increasingly casualties of the petrol price wars, and many are disappearing.

10

Life & Times

Snow clearance near the Grand Junction Inn, Sedgley, 1947.

Two photographs taken from the Inhedge in Upper Gornal. The Inhedge was a heavily populated area, now long-demolished and given over to new housing. The distant windows seen behind the boys are of Kent Street, Wesley.

Shown together in this second back garden shot, *c.* 1930, are Reg Reynolds, Lawson Reynolds, Rowland Lane, Billy Lane, and Mrs Bessie Wall, their grandmother.

A Christmas party organised by Harry
Jevon. It was held in the Working Men's
Hall, School Street, Sedgley.

Elias Henry Bevan of Shaw Road,
Coseley, poses proudly with his son
James Henry, aged about two, and not
yet shortened, on an equally proudly
owned bicycle around the year 1913.

In 1947 the area experienced very heavy snowfall. Here an attempt is being made to clear through from Tipton Street, Sedgley, to the main road.

The extent of drifting snow in Tipton Road near the junction with Gate Street.

A car lies buried and abandoned in Tipton Road. Woodsetton Lodge can be seen in the background. This must have been a familiar sight in the winter of 1947.

Four special constables relax in the coach as, duty over, and having walked a Council chairman to church, they await an easier journey home. The photograph was taken in about 1960.

Here the Civic Sunday parade, led by the Sedgley, Bilston and Coseley Special Constabulary, passes through Upper Gornal on its way to Zoar Chapel, Gornal Wood, *c.* 1959. The Council chairman is thought to have been Joe Jones who later became Mayor of Dudley, and whose civic service was also at Zoar. Leading the police procession are Vice Commandant Caswell of Coseley, leading the left-hand row. Two behind him is John Harris, also of Coseley. Second from the front in the middle row is Mr Field, First Commandant of Sedgley. Behind the group of bushes left can be seen the Upper Gornal Labour Club.

Another Civic Sunday parade, this time probably in 1958, passes through Sedgley Bullring to All Saints' Church, honouring Councillor Elsie Williams. Mrs Williams may just be seen in the centre of the second group. The coach was necessary as some police had come from a distance to swell the parade.

Sedgley Council House, in which both councillors would have served, on High Holborn. No longer used as such it is under some threat of obsolescence. Here it is still standing in 2001, with its future uncertain.

Sedgley Councillor Mrs Elsie Williams surveys her 'patch'. Mrs Williams was a very active councillor and pursued many causes including the creation of the Coronation Gardens, the Sedgley Pensioners Club in Ettymore Road, and the Quadrant Clinic on Beacon Estate. She was Chair of the Council in 1950 and 1958.

Bleak House Infant Welfare Centre and Clinic, Upper Gornal. Bleak House was demolished in 1968 and the service transferred to the Quadrant. Mrs Amy Matthews (caretaker), can be seen looking through the upstairs window on the right. The mothers with their prams seem to have dressed for the occasion.

Police Sergeant J.W. Marsh stands
in front of the sand-bagged door of
Sedgley police station in the
1940s.

For the Coronation of King George VI in 1936, many local celebrations were held. Here Sgt Marsh
leads the parade that has commenced in the grounds of Ellowes Hall. The Hall can just be seen in
the mists behind.

This collection of Sedgley advertisements from 1925 makes interesting reading. Many are well remembered by local folk or have contemporary relevance. J. Fellows and his family were pictured in *Sedgley & District* on page 94, standing in front of Bunker's Hill Toll House. Their farming was done on the land behind the Toll House.

Coseley Special Constable Terry Ratcliffe is seen here in 1966 receiving a Royal Society scroll from the Chairman of Coseley Council, Sidney Smart, for saving a local man's life. This must have been one of the last official events in Coseley Council House.

The long-standing centre of law and order for the parish was the Court House, Sedgley. Shown from this angle it is seen as a far older building to the rear than it appears from the front, and of stone. Cases were recorded there, and probably in an even earlier building too, from 1535. The present Magistrates Court was built nearby.

The opening of Sedgley Community Centre in 1986 and some of the Committee at the time. Facing camera, left to right: Marie Wall, Marie Bates, Edith Whitehouse, Vince Walters (partly hidden), Eileen Wright, and Ellis Wright.

A most important event in Sedgley was the changeover from gas street lighting to electric. The moment is captured here at Sedgley Council House in 1950 when, with Councillor Mrs E. Williams and others looking on, Chairman Jabez Fellows pushes the button to switch on the first electric street lights along the main road between Sedgley and Dudley. A local farmer, Councillor Fellows lived to 92 years of age.

11

Glimpses of the Past

This fossilised plant stem section from the coal measure forests was discovered in Lanesfield during pipelaying for the new water main from Beacon Sedgley Reservoir in the 1970s.

Sedgley Beacon crest, as many remember it, with the monument and the two water tanks, transferred from Brindley Heath's First World War POW camp in the 1920s to supply water to the northern end of Coseley. The first police mast has appeared by the time of this photograph from the late 1960s.

Many Mesolithic tools have been discovered just a short distance further north of the Beacon.

During the drought of 1976 these earthworks were noticed on the Beacon, near to the quarry. They resemble a gun emplacement: a Home Guard exercise of the Second World War period was one suggestion, but their origins remain a puzzle.

Andrew Barnett stands beside the unidentified earthworks at the northern end of Sedgley Beacon, so that the height of the rampart can be seen by comparison with himself.

Local artists and historians play a valuable part in recording our past. Here Ron Baker has taken a primitive sketch of the 1830s and enhanced it to show Five Ways, Lower Gornal, looking up Ruiton Street, at that date. The barn and cottages left have not yet become Five Ways Methodist Church.

Ron Baker's drawing of Straits Green, Lower Gornal, showing St Andrew's Mission, reminds us of an earlier, more rural prospect than the present.

The late Andrew Barnett's view of Christ Church, Coseley and the cricket field also reminds us of the earlier field name of the area, 'the Dimmocks'. This is now perpetuated in the name of a local avenue.

Andrew Barnett's reconstruction of cottages built in open land and away from metalled roads. This area had the appearance of rural countryside, though it was not far from heavy industry. This view is of Anchor Lane, Deepfields. Many older people remembered it as Richards's Cot.

This datestone, seen in the grounds of Rookery Hall, known now as The 44 Club, points to a previous date taken from deeds of a house that was here before it. An even earlier date is possible since the site fits very well with that of an early manor house for Ettingshall, sublet from the Lord of Sedgley Manor from before the Norman Conquest.

A detailed view of the stone wall of the Sedgley nail warehouse in Brick Street with its iron window frames. Now occupied by Cottage Blinds, it would have been built in the 1830s.

John Roper, Coseley historian, was the son of Joseph Roper, Clerk to Coseley Council. He was educated at Wolverhampton Grammar School, served in the Second World War and became a local solicitor in Bilston. He was a great contributor to the area's local history. He wrote much about Coseley, including the historic section of the Urban District's yearly handbook. His interests went much further afield and he produced books on the history of Wolverhampton, Dudley, and Sedgley. Many local archives benefited from John Roper's research over many years.

Walking the area is still a popular pursuit. This party on a local history walk take a rest in Turls Hill. Stan Dews, former Sedgley councillor, is sitting on the bench, left. This photograph was taken in the summer of 1987.

Sedgley Local History Society seen on their Millennium Summer Walk, in Townsend Avenue.

12

A Landscape of Contrasts

A row of interwar houses stand on Ladymoor Road, between the furnace slag of the old Coseley iron works, and the clouded horizon from Bilston steelworks, 1940s

A beautiful picture postcard view of one of the entrances to Baggeridge Woods, much loved by walkers and local people. This is how it appeared before the Second World War.

Lower Gornal, the Clee Hills and Shropshire countryside, seen from St James's churchyard in 1970, make an interesting contrast.

The beautiful Wishing Pool in Baggeridge Woods was a popular destination for walkers, and obviously a favourite postcard shot with John Price Printers, who produced cards from a variety of camera angles.

Between the late 1960s and the early 1970s the Northway Estate developed apace. Here, from an upper classroom window of Alder Coppice School, can be seen the spread of building into the farmlands behind by 1968. Some of these fields were known locally as being on the 'Seven Cornfields Walk'.

Frost makes this dramatic picture in Hodgins Field in Gospel End, 1976. A mixed shrub hedgerow, and evidence of ridge and furrow ploughing indicate the great age of the field.

Here, snow illuminates this recent evening photograph of the fields around Wood Farm, Gospel End, providing a further reminder that, where other chimneys have fallen, Baggeridge brickworks' stack still identifies a place of work.

The beautiful foliage seen here in this late 1930s postcard, could not hide the limestone fissure, a reminder of the great limestone extraction that had taken place on Wren's Nest, Woodsetton.

A view from houses in Bath Street, Sedgley, in 1947, showing the farm fields stretching to the Gorge at Hurst Hill, before the Gorge Estate was built.

ACKNOWLEDGEMENTS

The author acknowledges his gratitude to many people and sources of both pictures and information used in this book. Every effort has been made to contact all copyright holders of photographs where copyright has not originated with the person owning them.

Thanks are due to the Science Museum, London, the *Wolverhampton Express and Star*, the Black Country Society and Lanesfield Primary School. I thank Margaret Roper for her continuing interest and help and Ron Baker, who is constantly looking for fresh material and so frequently successful in his search.

Once again my own photographic collection has been supplemented by the collections of others, but the books would still not contain the interest and variety hoped for if it were not for so many people willing to lend some of their treasured possessions from the family camera, so that readers can share them, and their accompanying memories too.

My thanks go to: Des Allen, Vi Baker, Frances Barnett, Les Bates, Marie Bates, Joyce Beale, Joe Bradley, Kathleen Clark, Brian Cotterill, George Cox, Judith Craner, Ron Davies, the late Richard Dews, Mr W. D. Dowse, Mrs Angela Eades, Florence Edwards, Geoffrey Fellows, Gillian Fellows, the late E. Foulkes, Rita Forrest, Sylvia Genge, Peggy Gosling, Lily Gowland, Gwen Green, Mr. M.N. Hammond, Joe and Mary Harper, Evelyn Hill, John and Pam Hughes, Harry Jevon, Dorothy Johnson, Kit and Frank Jones, Angela Kiely, Les Mann, Gwen Marsh, David Melhuish, John Jones, John Newey, Laurence and Mary Nickolds, John and Rita Nickolds, Christina Nicholls, Diane Parkes, John Prince, Terry Ratcliffe, Brian Raybould, Tom Roberts, Mrs T. Shingler, Dorothy Sloan, Gladys Thomas, John and Marie Wakelam, Roy and Linda Watkins, Christine Wilkes, Fred Williams, Louis Willis, Margaret Wilson, Roger Wooldridge and, as always, the staff of Colab at Wolverhampton and Birmingham.

BRITAIN IN OLD PHOTOGRAPHS

Northamptonshire

Northampton Past & Present

Nottinghamshire

Arnold & Bestwood:
 A Second Selection
Kirkby in Ashfield:
 A Second Selection
Nottinghamshire at Work
Nottingham Past & Present

Oxfordshire

Around Abingdon
Around Didcot
Around Henley-on-Thames
Around Wheatley
Around Witney
Around Woodstock
Banbury
Banbury Past & Present
Cowley & East Oxford Past
 & Present
Forgotten Thames
Garsington
Henley-on-Thames Past &
 Present
Literary Oxford
Oxford
Oxfordshire at Play
Oxfordshire at School
Wantage, Faringdon & The
 Vale Villages
Witney

Shropshire

Shropshire Railways
South Shropshire
Telford

Somerset

Chard & Ilminster

Staffordshire

Aldridge Revisited
Kinver & Enville: A Second
 Selection

Newcastle-under-Lyme Past
 & Present
Pattingham & Wombourne
Stafford
Stoke-on-Trent Past &
 Present

Suffolk

Bury St Edmunds
Lowestoft Past & Present
Southwold
Stowmarket
Suffolk Transport
Suffolk at Work: A Second
 Selection

Surrey

Cheam & Belmont
Esher
Richmond
Walton upon Thames &
 Weybridge

Sussex

Around East Grinstead
Around Heathfield:
 A Second Selection
Bishopstone & Seaford:
 A Second Selection
Eastbourne Past & Present
High Weald: A Second
 Selection
Horsham Past & Present
Lancing
Palace Pier, Brighton
RAF Tangmere
Rye & Winchelsea

Tyne & Wear

Whitley Bay

Warwickshire

Around Leamington Spa
Around Leamington Spa:
 A Second Selection
Around Bulkington
Bedworth Past & Present
Knowle & Dorridge

Nuneaton Past & Present
Rugby: A Second Selection
Warwickshire Railways

West Midlands

Bilston, Bradley &
 Ladymoor
Birmingham Transport
Black Country Pubs
Blackheath
Cradley Heath
Cradley Heath: A Second
 Selection
Darlaston, Moxley &
 Bentley
Great Bridge & District
Halesowen: A Second
 Selection
Ladywood
Ladywood Revisited
Lye & Wollescote
Lye & Wollescote: A Second
 Selection
Northfield Past & Present
Oldbury
Rowley
Sedgley: A Fourth Selection
Smethwick
Solihull
Stourbridge, Wollaston &
 Amblecote
Stourbridge, Wollaston &
 Amblecote: A Second
 Selection
Tipton: A Third Selection
Wednesbury
Wordsley

Wiltshire

Around Devizes
Around Highworth
Castle Combe to
 Malmesbury
Crewkerne & the Ham
 Stone Villages
Marlborough: A Second
 Selection
Salisbury: A Second
 Selection

Worcestershire

Worcester Past & Present

Yorkshire

Around Hoyland
Around Hoyland: A Second
 Selection
Doncaster
Huddersfield
Huddersfield: A Second
 Selection
Leeds in the News
Northallerton: A Second
 Selection
Pontefract
Sheffield
Shire Green, Wincobank &
 Ecclesfield
Wombwell & Darfield

Wales

Anglesey
Carmarthen & the Tywi
 Valley
Chepstow & The River
 Wye
Haverfordwest
Milford Haven
Upper Teifi
Welshpool

Scotland

Annandale
Around Lochaber
Clydesdale
Musselburgh
Perth
Selkirkshire
St Andrews

Ireland

Coleraine & the Causeway
 Coast

To order any of these titles please telephone our distributor,
Haynes Publishing, on 01963 442105
For a catalogue of these and our other titles please telephone
Joanne Govier at Sutton Publishing on 01453 732423